# Being a Leader

## by Robin Nelson

first step nonfiction

Lerner Publications Company · Minneapolis

I can be a **leader.**

A good leader is
**responsible.**

A good leader follows rules.

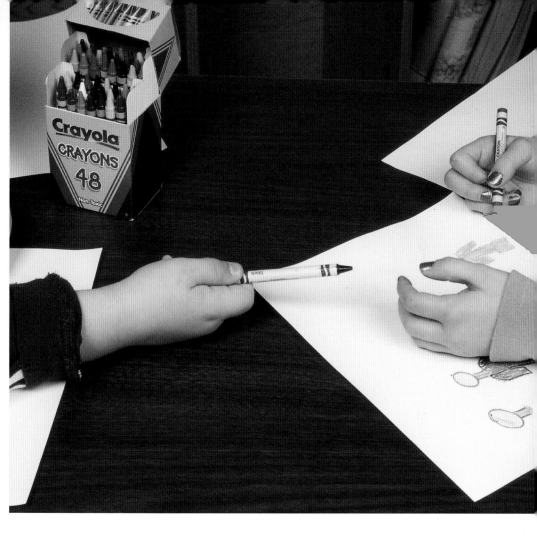

A good leader is **fair.**

A good leader **respects** others.

A good leader cares about others.

I can be a leader at school.

I can lead my class.

I can be a leader at home.

I can take care of my
sister or brother.

I can be a leader with my friends.

I can solve problems.

I can be a leader in my **community.**

I can help others.

I can be a good leader.

I can be a good example
for others.

# How can you be a leader at home?

- Teach your brother or sister something new.

- Help your mom and dad around the house.

- Clean your room without being asked.

- Teach your family a new game.

- Ask your family to volunteer to help others.

# How can you be a leader at school?

- Read a book to your class.

- Lead the Pledge of Allegiance.

- Help a younger student.

- Help a new classmate.

- Teach your class a new game.

- Lead a cleanup of your classroom or playground.

# Glossary

 **community** – the area where a group of people live

 **fair** – treating everyone the same

 **leader** – a person who shows the way

 **respects** – honors

 **responsible** – trustworthy, dependable

# Index

The photographs in this book are reproduced through the courtesy of: © Tom & Dee Ann McCarthy/CORBIS, front cover; © Betty Crowell, pp. 2, 22 (middle); © Tom McCarthy/TRANSPARENCIES, Inc., pp. 3, 22 (bottom); © Richard Hutchings/CORBIS, p. 4; © Todd Strand/Independent Picture Service, pp. 5, 13, 15, 22 (second from top); © Jack McConnell, pp. 6, 22 (second from bottom); © CORBIS Royalty-Free, p. 7; © Bill Bachmann/TRANSPARENCIES, Inc., p. 8; © Tom and Dee Ann McCarthy/TRANSPARENCIES, Inc., p. 9; © S. Grant/TRIP, pp. 10, 14, 22 (top); © Rubberball Productions, p.11; © Ed Kashi/CORBIS p. 12; © J.E. Glenn/TRANSPARENCIES, Inc., p. 16; © Michael Moore/TRANSPARENCIES, Inc., p. 17.

Illustrations on pages 19 and 21 by Tim Seeley.

Lerner Publications Company
A division of Lerner Publishing Group, Inc.
241 First Avenue North
Minneapolis, MN 55401 U.S.A.

Website address: www.lernerbooks.com

Library of Congress Cataloging-in-Publication Data

Nelson, Robin, 1971–
    Being a leader / by Robin Nelson.
        p.    cm. — (First step nonfiction)
    Includes index.
    Summary: An introduction to leadership at school, at home, with friends, and in the community, with specific examples of how to be a leader at home and school.
    ISBN-13: 978–0–8225–1287–5 (lib. bdg. : alk. paper)
    ISBN-10: 0–8225–1287–4 (lib. bdg. : alk. paper)
    1. Leadership—Juvenile literature. [1. Leadership.] I. Title. II. Series.
HM1261 N45  2003
303.3'4—dc21                                                             2002000609

Manufactured in the United States of America
8 – DP – 10/1/12